Letters from the 1

Acknowledgements

Special thanks to Ian and Val Horn
for all their help and encouragement.

LETTERS FROM THE TRENCHES

Cyril Morrell

Edited by Kathleen Carter

BREWIN
BOOKS

First Published by
Brewin Books, Studley, Warwickshire
in March 2000
www.brewinbooks.com

ISBN 1 85858 163 X

British Library Cataloguing in Publication Data
A Catalogue record for this book is available from
the British Library

Typeset in Palatino and
made and printed in Great Britain by
SupaPrint (Redditch) Ltd
Redditch, Worcestershire.
www.supaprint.com

Contents

Introduction   vi

The Letters   1

Illustrations   26 - 40

The Morrell Family   68

INTRODUCTION

The following pages describe the experiences and emotions witnessed by Pte T C Morrell of 10th Batt E Yorks Regiment as recorded in his own words through his letters home to his parents and family during the first world war.

He died on 12th March 1917 at the age of 23 yrs in the battlefields of France when fighting for "Good old England" and his family at home.

He was my uncle and, although we never met as his early death prevented such a union, by reading his words and learning about him from the remaining members of his beloved family I feel I knew him myself. His fragile and faded letters are written on rough paper, mainly in pencil and by dim candlelight on his "can".

I have copied his words exactly as he wrote them, including any grammatical errors and spelling mistakes as I feel they all contribute to the personality which emerges. Despite their imperfections each letter is a literary masterpiece in its own right because of the feelings they evoke through their simplicity.

The letters reveal a naivety, a purity and a figure of innocence and acceptancy who tried hard to be cheerful in an attempt to protect his beloved mother from her fears.

I feel that he believed, to a degree, that he was protected by his faith in God and, whatever happened, it was God's will that it should be so. At one point he even indicated pity for his enemy, fearing that the German troops were perhaps being as badly treated as he and his comrades.

He died a Private. No metal badges or medals for bravery and, his most precious legacy, a simple woollen scarf knitted by his six year old sister who was always remembered at the end of his letters home with added "kisses" until the paper ran out.

But by reading his words, to me, Uncle Cyril has become a true hero of that dreadful war.

He epitomizes the ordinary "Tommy" who was forced to sacrifice his life so that the likes of me could hopefully lead a better life in a future world. Although I am already twice the age of my soldier uncle at his death, I feel strangely inexperienced when I consider the wisdom shown in his attitude towards the difficulties life presented to him, and also extremely privileged to have felt an intimate contact with such a truly gentle man. Perhaps one day I shall even visit the patch of ground once marked by a "durable wooden cross" to guard his remains and thank him personally. Who knows. But I already feel that part of his spirit is written like his words deep within me.

Three final letters from his pals continue to tell the story of Cyril after his premature death, and finalise the brief history of Mrs Morrell's gallant soldier.

There would, I am sure, have been more letters, but some have got lost through the passage of time and others, perhaps, censored. These are the only ones remaining – locked away for safe-keeping in his "box", cherished by his broken-hearted mother, later by his little sister, and now in my hands. I shall continue to treat them with the respect they deserve, and I shall feel eternal gratitude for a man who's gentle nature has given me so much to contemplate and be thankful for.

Cyril's six year old sister (my mother), is now in her 90th year and still sleeps with his photograph by her bedside – he remains her loving brother.

For Cyril.

xxxxxxxxxxxxxx

Cyril Morrell

THE LETTERS

Company M
Withernsea Camp, Yorkshire.

June 14th 1916.

Dear Father and Mother,

I was very pleased to see you had not forgot the parcel. It was gladly received, I can tell you. Of course the cakes were A1 and the fakes came in useful, it will save me buying for a bit. I gave all the chaps in my tent a cake, so you can gess they did not last long, there are fourteen of us as you know.

Leslie's little trouble has worried you a bit. I should think he will not do such soft things again, it might have been worst. Tell Dad we got no holiday on monday. I should think these last few days have had it in for us – it has been all work.

I had a letter from Mr Page this morning, we are always looking out for letters or parcels, you can tell it is ten past six and I have just had time to read it. If we are not on drill, we are cleaning our buttons or shoes, and they have wanted it to. The weather from friday till this morning it has been rotton -- all rain, but a little drier this afternoon for a good job.

We all went on parade to the pleasure grounds were they had a meeting with Lord Kitchener There were about two thousand there with three bands they played the dead march and several other things – it was very nice but would have been better if it had been warmer, that was on Monday night after our drill time so I could not write you before.

Leslie asked if there were plenty of nice girls here, but I have not seen any yet.

You said you had a ring paper the other day, well I think you should see Mr Page about it, you will get more added on to that most certainly, do not be slow, I can not do anything with it myself now. I have done all I can and it has been a bother, but dont worry over me. We had a lot more men come up here this morning from Lichfield barracks but they soon turned them back, there is no room, so I suppose they would go back to Lichfield.

Be sure you tell them the truth about what you had off me because I have

1

told them at Lichfield that I allowed you sixteen shillings a week. Soon chaps have got to appear in a day or so for cheating the government. Well I have it to you, I have been worrying about that whether you took any notice about what Mrs Tivey said. You know she said you are soft not to add another shilling or two on, do not say anything about I have menchand her name will you?.

Well I must close, with love to all, from your loving son,

CYRIL.   For "K" xxxxxxxxxxxxxxxxxxxxxxxx

Company M
Withernsea Camp Yorkshire.

June 21st 1916.

Dear Mother,

I was glad to hear Lillian is better and Mr Adams has been about the money so that is done with.

Well it has been my washing day today and I have been washing my shirt out. The one that I brought with me. I cannot wear the shirts the army supply, so I want you to send me another one from home. Of course I have worn the army shirts for a week or so but I have been in pain they have rubbed me that much that I have been pink all over -- it is the truth. The other chap's shirts are not as rough as mine, but I can keep the army shirts with me and the sleeves are about six inches to long, they keep getting below my jacket.

You need not trouble about the money to send it, take it out of my box however much it costs. If you roll it up and put brown paper round it it will be allright.

Well I am trudging along so do not worry. I shall be over soon. I have my supper every night so it takes some money. I tell you what it takes us. We have to buy soap and toothpaste, soldiers paste for his buttons, some brown stuff for belts and my word, a penny cake's three pence here, and we have got to buy a stick to walk out with, I expect they think it is something to take care of me.

Well I have not been out tonight, so I thought I would have my supper and write a letter on my can.

I had a letter from Auntie Alice on Monday, she said she is going to write me every week, they are as well as you can expect -- she is in a rut.

I wrote to Phil and he has answered me, and the letter I wrote Auntie Mary, but I have not had a letter back yet from her. And I also wrote to Mr Holden but had no reply, I cannot seem to think they have had them somehow.

Well I wish you goodnight, hoping all are in good health from your loving son

CYRIL

Tell Dad in a week we have got to go to York for shooting for a day or so.

For Kathleen xxxxxxxxxxxxxxxxxxxxxxxxxx

3

Withernsea.   June 24th 1916.

Dear Dad,

I am getting over my operation allright but I have got to have another poke tomorrow and then I shall know when I am coming back to Bilston, so cheer up it wont be long.

Well I am going on allright so far.

We went to the sea yesterday for a bath, but it was chilly. There is a nice old lot of us too.

We have the band every bathing parade. I expect it is the band to awake people up to come and look at us.

We have an officer with us he has rose from the ranks he is a good sort. He took us for a route march on Thursday about 10 miles, it was a treat, and he gave us 10 mins in every hours march. He said - now my lads, you need not kill yourselves- take it easy- so you can tell what sort he is.

I am in officers mess this morning and we get plenty of crocks to wash, of course we take it in turns so I might not have it again for a month.

Well I'm glad to hear Theo has got on allright at last, now he wants to keep his job so that the government will have no claim on him - he would not like the army I am sure.

Will write again before I come over. We are just off for breakfast, it is fish this morning- not eggs, but we got eggs (no bacon).

I went to the pictures last night but it was not as good as Wood's pictures. Sometimes when you have got Answers paper to spare, let me have one. I do not want you to send it every week, but occasionally. Auntie Alice asked me if I should like a paper every week, but they do not have Answers, so I told her not to send any, very kind of her I am sure. Well she said she will write me every week so I shall look for her letters.

There is some smart ones in M Camp, some of them are too slow to carry dinners so we call ourselves the "mug" camp not a bad name is it?

I have had to use my tooth brush for my buttons, so when you send me a new one I can swill my new one out.

It is not a very nice morning this morning. It is raining. It is like a mud puddle when it rains but the winds soon dry it up. We got another week's wages yesterday - three shillings, I do not know how to spend it. I expect you will be pleased to hear I have had no beer, while I have been here-- I do not want any. The chaps call me soft- but they can go on with it.

Well I must close, hoping all are in good health as it leaves me at present. From you loving son

CYRIL.

Kathleen, xxxxxxxxxxxxxxxxxxxxx

Withernsea.

Dear Mother,

I am sending you one or two things I bought the other day. The shirt will come in useful for Theo or Dad and the brushes are always useful.

I thought you were not going to send me my shirt so the men are always selling clothes, so the shirt is not an army shirt so I bought it, I thought it would come in useful.

Well I had another letter from Auntie Alice and one post-card from Richard so I had a bit of news. I hear you went to Clent on Saturday so things seem to be looking up. I dont blame you for going. Did you take Kathleen with you ?.

Well about sending cakes, I think stamps will do better because I am always writing and it does take some money a week. I'm glad I do not depend on the army pay. I do not know were I should be.

I am very glad Theo has made a start at work. It has been a worry to him but never mind.

Mother I have no tooth comb, that would be very useful, although I have not needed one yet, but we never know.

I have had a letter from Mr Holden on Sunday- I thought he had forgotten me.

It is allright about the money the sargent major said to me the other day that your mother will pick up 9/2d a week so it is funny you have not received any yet - you may pick it up in the lump.

Very pleased to hear Lillian has got her 1st class certificate for cookery.

I had my 2nd inoculation yesterday afternoon but I have got over it so far. It gives you some gipp I can tell you Two of our chaps had no sleep yesterday night, they were groaning all night long. But you need not trouble about my arm. It is only a bit stiff today- of course we have another 24hrs off- a good job it is raining so I am writing in the tent on my can.

Tell Uncle John the razor is O K. It was a spendid present to give me. We are allowed to wear all underclothes and socks as long as you make full kit bag. You must not have anything missing on kit inspection and then they do not say anything.

You have been busy at home with bricklayers and carpenters. What are you doing, getting the house ready incase I come home ?.

Well I have said all this time thanking you very much for the shirt and other things. I sent you this shirt so you can wash it out. Well it is a good one for sixpence and those brushes. Don't you think so ?

I shall manage with two shirts now, one to wash and one to wear. You should see me washing What Ho!

When I send for any money do not delay it because they only give us two days notice to get some and if I have got none I cannot come over so has soone as I write for some let me have it.

Well you will have to excuse me starting again on the letter, but this is all this time. Hoping you are all well in health as it leaves me at present. From your loving son,

CYRIL

For "K" xxxxxxxxxxxxxxxxxxxxxx

Withernsea Camp.

Dear Mother and Dad,

pleased to hear you received my parcel allright. Yes, I received your parcel allright.

Tell Harold I was very pleased with the fags, they will come in I can tell you. Also the stamps.

I see by your letter the allotment is allright- - I thought you would have it soon.

Well I have had a letter from Auntie Mary, she has been through it. Well I do not blame her. She said she is feeling a lot better - so her letter said, and the family, for a good job.

I have got to stop in camp tonight and guard the tents, we have got some old stagers up here, they know the game for stealing so we take it in turns. Well you had better send me another half-soverign so I shall have it in readiness. Let me have it as soon as you can.

I had a letter from Mrs Tivey today and I have wrote her back.

It is washing day for me today, I have been washing my socks and shirts. We have to do them when we have got time--- so you can see.

Well, I have said all this time. Hoping all are well in health as it leaves me at present.

From you loving son,

CYRIL.

"K"

xxxxxxxxxxxxxxxxxxxxxxxx

7

T.C. MORRELL. Comp M Batt 3
Withernsea Camp. Yorkshire.

Reg East York
July 6th 1916.

Dear Mother and Father,

I have not received any money yet, have you sent it for I need to get it for Friday morning, if so I shall get it tomorrow and I have had a disappointment today.

We were to come on Saturday - but have been put back till next Saturday - - the rotton dogs. Well one thing and another, I felt a bit worried, I have been vaccinated today and you see if I had come over this week-end my arm would have been allright, but as it is now it will be at its worse for next Saturday, that is the 15th and if it is I shall stop here and fall sick and then come on Tuesday.

I heard from Richard this morning, but had no letter from you. Have you all forgot me this week ?.

Well I thought I was allright till six tonight-- and I do not care a button for anyone in the army. Some chaps have only been here three weeks and are going home on leave on Saturday. I went to the sagent and tolled him, but you may as well save your breath and put up with it.

If our Theo joins he wants a good horse whiping - they can do what they like with you.

Of course I am very wicked tonight, so do not take any notice of me, what I am saying.

Well I thought I would let you know, so I have wrote you straight away, well, I shall get over my wickedness in the morning - so do not worry about me we all have these times now and again, so good- night hoping all are in the pink as it leaves me in health,

From you loving son,   CYRIL.

I will write later,

For "K" xxxxxxxxxxxxxxxxxxxxxxxx

Withernsea Camp, Yorkshire.   July 8th 1916.

Dear Mother,

I have received the two letters allright, also the note, I was sorry to disapoint on Saturday but I cannot help it.

I was wicked when they said we have put you back for a bit. There are three in our camp with me to have a furlow, but they have only got to go to Birmingham. If I had come over on Saturday I should have had a pal all the way- - he lives in Tettenhall.

Well I have got it over now- - so I will send a post -card before I come, so has to let you know for shure. I think it is very kind of you for sending money out of my allotment but you would be surprized the money it takes a week.

Pleased to hear that Dad has plenty of work. I hope his health will not take him, he is not so young as he used to be, thats what I mean.

I see Harold and Lillian is going to Worcester today - - good luck to them. Fancy Elsie Hammonds leaving school so soon. I hope she will stop with you so you can get out for a bit.

How is Leslie behaving himself ? I hope he is a good lad to you and Dad, he can take it from me, he would not like the army, there is too many bosses. He would soon get in clink if he answered them back even.

It is a place on the field covered in barbed wire, and military police guarding day and night with loaded guns, also dogs trained for that purpose- - so it is even worse than ordinary police stations. And if they are shouting, they lie them down to the floor for four hours at a time. Will you tell him to be a good lad, I should like a line from him any time he as an hour to spare.

I was very sorry to hear the bad news of the Bilston people passing away. Tell Theo, I send my deepest sympathy to Mrs Bayliss and family. It is a trouble to them, but it is a thing we have all got to come to.

But I am not surprised so much of Dr Kendrick's death, he looked like death when he was going away in the cab. I saw him myself.

Well, I could scrat my arm off, it does itch, it is the vaccination working up, but it will be at its worst next Saturday, and if it is the only thing is to come on Tuesday, What do you think ?

Well, I will let you know later how it is going on. I think I have said all this time. Hoping all are in the pink, with much love to all, from your loving son,

CYRIL

Kathleen xxxxxxxxxxxxxxxxxxxxxxx

9

Withernsea Camp. July 25th 1916.

Dear Sister,

Well I told you I would send you a dog -biscuit to try them and let me know how you like it- - give them all a taste at home.

Very pleased the weather is allright at Bilston, it has been showers and thunderstorms here.

How did you enjoy going out with the Sunday school children?. It is quite a treat to you but I am having too much.

Well Lloyd George said in this mornings paper that the war will be over this year- - I hope he is telling the truth.

I went to the Y M C A hut the other night and a very nice jolly lady came up to me and we were talking for a bit and she said I have some small testaments in my bag- - should you like one, so I said Yes I should. Well she gave another one to a lad who is in our tent and asked us to go to their house for tea sometime, I said we shall see.

We are having plenty to eat so far, but I always want a bit of money for case I should not have enough, so if Mother recieves my parcel tell her to send me the ammount I paid for them if she can, I am sure she will not grumble.

Tell Kathleen, I recieved her letter and I might be coming to see her some week-end. It is a rush, but I should have Sunday with you. Of course it wont be yet a bit but you must look forward to it.

I am helping the cooks today, it is a mucky job but we must not grumble it is all keeping me away from the front so I dont care.

Could you send me a little drop of petrol in a glass bottle, it is in the stable in a large glass bottle and some of that stuff to clean my buttons in another glass bottle- - pack them up as they wont break.

Well I must close, hoping all are in good health,

From your loving brother, CYRIL

Kathie. xxxxxxxxxxxxxxxxxxxxxx

Withernsea Camp

(I forgot to say, we had to turn out on Monday night, but did not come our way after all).

Dear Leslie,

When am I going to have a letter from you ? I am still waiting so do not forget to write me.

We are having very hot weather now, it is really too hot if anythink.

Tell Lillian I received the parcel but had no time to write back straight away as I was doing a bit of washing and had a bath so you can see how busy I was.

I have received also the money order Mother sent me for the pants but forgot to say anythink about it in my letters.

I only received two shillings last Friday and still the sargent major said I was some more in debt. I do not know, nor any of the other chaps how we have got in debt, but it is no use asking about it as they can do as they like with you.

Well we were to have three shillings one week and four another, but we have not seen four yet, so I am afraid you will have to send me some,or some fags.

I am writing to Mother as well in this letter, so you can all read it. I hope you will keep your job and be a good lad to your mother. I am sure you would not like this life at all.

Well Leslie we had a worse night than that one at Bilston with the Zepps. will just tell you all about it.

On Friday night we went to bed as usual and about two hours later when we was asleep and I was very comfortable that night, the sargent major came round to all the tents and shouted to us all- - all men get dressed and get up to the lines with all our equipment on. Well it had been very hot that day but it got very foggy at night it was a sea-fog and you could not see your hand before you. Well we got dressed somehow, and got to our lines. We only had 10 mins to do everythink and we had to march about a mile up the road away from the camp with one blanket and oil- sheet. We went to bed on the roadside but we could not sleep on account of the noise. The sargent major was frightened and he thought our times had come but it passed over without any damage at all at Withernsea for a good job and we stoped there till about 5 O'clock and they did not have morning parade-- I mean first think.

We went on drills at nine O'clock that was the only one quarter since I have joined up. Well we needed it, what do you say ?

I expect you read the damage elsewhere what they done.

I have got to be careful what I write, on account of the post office opening them- - we have been warned.

Tell Mother and Dad not to worry about me. I shall be allright.

Well lad be good, I might come over any week-end if Mother will let me have some money, which she will I am sure.

Hoping you are in the pink of health, with love to all from your loving brother,

CYRIL

Cowden Camp

Dear Leslie,

I thought you would like a few words from me. How are your girls going on ? Has she still got her hair down her back. I hope you are a good lad to your parents and are not teazing the dog while I am away. How does the work go down with you lately, you dont write me a lot but I expect it is a little lady that you have got and I expect she keeps you out late at night.

Well it is raining very hard today and I am orderly man, that is, serving the meals out today. It is a rotton job, but we all have it in our turns, but we shall be having a big markey put up next week and then that job will be allright.

There came another thirty men up here last week, so that makes about a hundred and twenty men how here.

I am sending a few fakes pictures for Kathleens book-- tell her she must save them, then I will get some more of the same kind, they are well known boxers and I will try to get the series of them.

I had a nice little walk last night, but it is a little to far for us to go every night. We went to different places about town, and the rain kept off until we got back to camp, and then it has kept on till now.

The place was Hornsea. I have sent Kathleen a picture post-card which I hope she will get.

You never said that Miss Holden was getting married, but I get a little news by this account from someone else.

We were to have gone to chapel this morning, but it is raining too hard and the chapel is at Hornsea-- five miles away, we have to start at eight O'clock to get there. Shall be delighted to hear from you, hoping all are in the pink, as it leaves me at present, from your loving brother,

CYRIL.

Cowden Camp.

Dear Mother,

I expect you think I have forgotten you this week, but you see I have been waiting for the sargent to say whether or not I have got a pass this week. Well as far as I know I have, but cannot say now whether I shall be able to come because they are sorting all of us with traids out and I might be sent to work somewhere before Saturday, and that is how I am placed.

I am as you will see placed very hawkward. Well if I do come it might be only 48hrs has the chaps have spoilt it stopping over their leave and some of them have not come back since last Saturday yet, and now the leave is from 12 A M Saturday till 12A M Monday, it is not enough for me, you see if I start at 12 on Saturday, it means about 11 O'clock on Saturday evening before I can get home and then I shall have to start back on Monday morning at 4 A M. Thirteen and six, it will take for one day at home and that will be just the Sunday.

You see I cannot let you know for certain, now this job has proped up about being sent to work for I might have the news any time before Saturday.

Well I have got to, go but the only thing is to waite and see, I should like to come before I am moved. It is a confounded nuisant being pushed about.

I had a letter from Auntie Elsie and Uncle John, so if you see them before Saturday, dont tell them I am coming, dont tell anyone till I come. For if you tell them I shall not come.

I was going to order a fowl tonight, but I shall have to let it go this time owing to this trouble.

I think my luck is out with passes and then again having one for shure this week and then this confounded 48 hrs props up. Well if I come I shall stop till Monday dinner before going back and they can send me to "You Know". -- I have never had a crime against me yet but if they do not get the time altered for us I shall have one.

I heard that Auntie Alice had been over to Bilston and lots of other news, and that the military authorities has give him till the end of this year, well, that is a good job, but it would have been a better job if he had got out of it all together. What do you say ??.

I think this is all the Cowden news now. No, I forgot to tell you we had the Zepps over on Monday and we have one or two guns working for them next time.

I had to dress and go on cliff patrol for four hours before the bounders came, we also have the search-lights here and they were a treat the other night they had them on.

I believe they made a mess at Nottingham, all one street practical all down.

I think this is all this time, hoping you are in the best of health as it leaves me at present, and thank the Lord for that. I have had a nice face, but dont worry, it is allright again now with the tooth-ache.

From your loving son,

CYRIL
I will try to do my best to come.

Kathleen. xxxxxxxxxxxxxxxxxxxxx

POST CARD
(A Daily Mail Battle picture)   3rd Oct 1916.

To Miss K Morrell (aged six years)

Dear Sister,

I have arrived quite safely and I got in camp at a right time so I am quite
allright and we are having it very wet here today. I will write you a letter
later on so so long, from your loving brother,

                                        CYRIL. xxxxxxxxxxxxxxxxx

Cowden Camp.

Dear Sister,

I have received your letter today Tuesday, I thought you had forgotten to write me. I expect it does not seem so long I was over-- but it does to me. Well, I threw two live bombs last Friday, so we have done with that course.

I am about sick of what we are doing up here now, same thing over and over again.

Fancy Harold scalding his foot- - I am sorry to hear that, I will write to him later.

It will be rotton as the winter comes on up here, it will be all drills and bed.

The next time you write me, put a small looking glass in as I am without one- - any old thing will do.

Hope Leslie will go on allright once more, and tell him what I asked him on the station, to write me.

How did Kathleen like the post-card I sent her? I am writing this with camp light and sitting on a bed so you can partly tell after gas-light it is rotton.

Well I think I have said all this time-- thanking you for the letter.

Hoping you are all well in health as it leaves me at present.

From your loving brother,

CYRIL.

Kathleen. xxxxxxxxxxxxxx
xxxxxxxxxxxxxx
xxxxxxxxxxxxxx

(I think you had better share them among yourselves.)

GOOD NIGHT.

Reply to-
    Pte T C M 25934

    Batt 2 guns Regt East York,
    Stationed at Cowden Camp
    Nr Hornsea.

                                                    Oct 20th 1916.

Dear Theo,

I got the parcel today, Friday and I thank you for the looking-glass and sigs. Tell Mother I recieved the money note allright and the fags and the papers. The gloves will come in handy for these cold nights. I must thank Auntie for knitting me them when I write her again. I also got Lilian's post -card and tell Mother if Kathleen's bad, I mean very bad, don't forget to send me a note. I shall soon be over to Bilston but I hope you will not have to send me on that sort of thing.

Well the note I received today I am very glad it as come, as I have sent my suit to be washed and I have been spending my money on food. If Lillian's making cake- ask her to send me some - - I don't mean every week, but sometimes and I will write to Harold the next letter.

Sorry I have left it so long but I have not had many letters from Bilston for this last two weeks

I have asked Richard to remind the people at home about writing me.

Dear Theo, you stick to your job and old on with all your might or else you will soon get sick of what I have gone through. It is rotton up here, but I would rather stop here for Leslie and you, rather than you should come up.

The dark nights and stoping up all night to guard the coast is no soft job. Leslie knows that if you ask him.

Well I must close, hoping all are in the pink, thanking all for the parcel they have sent me.

Tell Dad he must write sometimes as I am often thinking about him and all at home. Well I send by best love to all, I remain your loving brother,

                            CYRIL.

Cowden Camp (The little wooden hut.)   15th Nov 1916.

Dear Mother and Dad,

I received your letter yesterday and also the blades that Uncle John done up.

Well I am sorry to say that it does not look like me being over before X-Mas. We do get disappointed in the army and we have to put up with it. Tell Kathleen not to mind as Cyril will be coming to stop with her for 5 days soon.

Have you heard anythink from Mrs Tivey or have you fell out ? She has not written to me yet and I shan't write her again till I have a line from her.

We are having a few nice days, but I must not crack it up or else it might start to rain again.

Fancy "K" stating to nitt so soon- - she is a knock-out. I often look at her before going to sleep at night and wondering if she is in bed, as we go to bed about seven thirty now the nights are drawing in.

It gets worse up here being no life about out-side. I went to Oldbury last night, it takes me about an hour and a half to get to this place walking it and they have a Y M C A. there.

Well we just dropped in the Y M , and they were having a concert, but we had no time to hear anythink, only we had somethink to eat and it was time to start back again. I can tell you I was soon asleep when I got back.

Well Dad, it looks as if we have all got to do somethink to help this war to finish- - you are working over and I think myself if they capture any more Germans as they have been doing, we shall soon have it over.

I was told by some of the East-Yorks that they are making headway all along the line, and if they can only keep it up we shall have it finished the starting of next year, and they have all been out.

Well, I must close, hoping all are in the best of health- sorry I cant come, but you must keep on smiling, from your loving son,

                    CYRIL.   Kathleen xxxxxxxxxxxxxxxxx

Cowden Camp.   Dec 1st 1916.

Dear Lillian,

I expect you have thought I have forgotten you all, well Lillian, I never saw a sight like I did on 27th November, we have the air-craft men in the next field to us and the Zepps came but it was a picture to see the search-lights on him, he stud still in the air for five minutes and the Zepp also turned round and the air-craft men were firing at him all the time- - we thought we were on the battlefield at last.

They were dropping bombs all the time and the guns in the next field were going off- - it was a noise.

Well the cliffs were jumping all the way around us, but it done no damage here, we found about six bombs that had not gone off.

Well, the one got Scott free and another came, the men hit it on the tail-end, and it dropped several foot, but the search-lights followed it straight out to sea- that must have been the one that came down. I was on guard at the time, so you see I saw everythink that was going on.

Well I should have wrote you before, but I thought it was best to let things die down a bit. I thought they might open the letters. I would not have missed it for six shillings!

You know what it was at Bilston when they came, but how should you like them so near as we had them.?

Well Lillian we are being examined on Monday by the Doctor, to see whether we are fit once more. I will let you know how I get on.

I had a parcel from Auntie Alice today, and some of the things were missing. It had been crushed and broken open.

You see in your parcel a little broach inside it, it is for Kathleen and say whether you would like one- - I am sure Kathleen will be delighted with it.

How do you like this, I had a letter from Harold on Wednesday- but you need not say anythink about it to anyone I will show it to you when I come home.

Well Lillian, I think I have said all this time, hoping to hear from you soon, and I hope you are all in the pink at home,

From your loving brother,

CYRIL.

I am hoping to see you all soone, shall send you a photo.
For Kathleen xxxxxxxxxxxxxxxxxxxxxx
(Let her wear the broach .)

Pte T C M 25394
Comp A 2nd Garrison E Yorks
Cowden Camp Nr Hornsea.

Dec 6th 1916.

Dear Mother,

I received Lillians letter and will write to him (Harold) soon.

Well I expect you will not like the news- - but I have passed A1, yesterday I went infront of the Doctor and was passed B1 but the travelling board today have passed me fit.

Well dear Mother, dont worry yet, because I shall have to go through my training again and very likely I shall not pass.

Keep it quite, I will not tell anybody- - I have had my name down again for my trade, I expect it is behind paper after all.

Well, how do you like my photo ? I have spoilt the other from Phil, they got all over fat somehow - but thesees have been taken at Hornsea.

I have not received my parcel yet, and that letter that Leslie wrote me came on the 4th December - so you see they get mis-laid. How is my little girl going on? I am longong to see her and all of you once more.

I dread training again, it is the only thing that worries me. I dont mind going to, France - but its going under that Tommy- Rott again.

I will write you again soon about the X-mas passes, the only thing I know about them, they start on 18th December, but know this board as come it might upset everythink.

Well I think I have said all this time, at least I think I had not aught to have tolled you, but cheer up Mar, I must close now, hoping all are in the pink as it leaves me at present from your loving son,

CYRIL.

"K" xxxxxxxxxxxxxxxxx xxxx

Pte 25349
Cowden Camp, Nr Hornsea.   Dec 7th 1916.

Dear Sister,

well I am glad you found my last letter interesting - but how do you like the other letter ?

You will find I have sent 10/6 in orders, I want you to cash them and put it on one side so that any time I want any to send me some.

I have got pretty well of money with me now if I come on pass, but have you seen the papers about not letting the men come home, only on draught pass. I think they are doing as they like - the rotton dogs. But I will let you know about whether we are having one a bit later.

Well sister, I have received the parcel allright and I will write to Auntie Meg and send her my photo. I am having some more done and I will do my best to get you a brooch and some china - but I went to several shops last week and they had none, so I will try my luck again.

How does Dad like me? Ask him if it will do for a fit man. When I come I will bring the letter that Harold wrote me- but it is not much to see.

Yes sister it was a wonderful sight that Zepp - but we dont want them so near again. They only dropped about 40 bombs that's all - you can gess how the earth shook - but thank the Lord no damage was done.

We all expect to be moved to the 3rd Batt soon, so if we do before X-mas our passes will be off.

Thank Theo for the fags and sweets - they are a treat and my cold is wonderfully better - those sweets will about finish it off.

Yes, a lovely bunch of grapes were spoilt in that parcel Auntie Alice sent me, but never mind - better luck next time.

I heard from Richard today so I shall have to write him.

Well, dear sister, I must close thanking all at home for the parcel.

I am writing in the candle-light - so you can see its very nice after gas - but cheer and I will do my best to come and see you once more.

The reason I am sending money home is to save a little, and you tell Mother and Dad not to worry as I have plenty with me. I had two good weeks - I picked up 5/- twice. Well I must thank you for the second time, hoping all are in the pink as it nearly leaves me,

From your loving soldier-boy,

CYRIL.

Let me know if you receive the notes straight away.

How much have I got in the Sunday school club?? Let me know.

Cowden camp.

Dear Sister,

thanks vey much for your letter this week. I would like you to write every week like that. I also received Kathleen's P C this morning, sorry to hear that Dad is bad, I hope he will soon get right again - it is rotton at Christmas time.

Yes, the bonus will come in handy for you, I do hope you will get it. Well I do not know when I am coming home again - we might get Christmas passes yet, but this morning I have had a bit of good news - I am going to go for a trade- test, I dont know how I shall get on and cant say when I am going, but its in the orders so I dont think it will be long.

Well the papers have a bit of good news also, but I think its only bluff. When you send another letter, I want you to put some shirting in, I want to patch my shirt, so dont forget it will you?

I am sending you another photo, you can have it, and what number is Auntie Sarah? I want to send her one.

Yes, the Doctor said I wanted some teeth, but he can go on with it, I can chew the leather that we get for biscuits, so I think they will do for a bit longer.

Well Lillian I am asking you whether you would send Faney a photo or not, write soon and let me know. I dont want Theo to know I have asked you such a thing, for he may not like it.

I get pretty well of letters from her, but I have one to answer now but I dont like them to come so quick, so I am keeping it for a bit later. Dont tell Theo!

Well, tell Dad I am feeling A1, but we must waite later and see what I am going to do. I hope he is better by the time you get this letter. I am often thinking of you all and hope that if I don't get home for Christmas that you will all enjoy yourselves and dont think of troubling about me. I shall be allright, I am still in England yet so dont worry. Well dear sister, I must close with fondest love, hoping all are in the pink as it leaves me at present, from your loving brother,

CYRIL.

Give "K" theses for me. xxxxxxxxxxxxxxxxxxxxxx

I hope you get the photos allright. Excuse the scribble as I am trying to catch the post.

Withernsea. (14, Young St)   Dec 16th 1916.

Dear Mother and Dad,

I expect you will be surprized to hear that I am in this dirty old spot, Withernsea. My trade test has gone west owing to me being marked "A". You will find my address at the top, and dont make any mistake addressing the letter.

I could not write any sooner as we got ready on Thusday to come here, but was cancelled and we thought we were not coming till after X-Mas then, but as you see I am here as we had new equipment today- - so you see we have been busy cleaning it.

I expect Auntie Alice has sent me a parcel today for my birthday- - it is a funny one this time, but never mind, we must still hope for the best.

They are sending 400 out on Tuesday, and we are starting those rotten route marches again. They are passing hundreds of young chaps for the front, well this place is full of men. I never thought I would see this place again while I am soldiering, but we never know do we ?.

I should have wrote you before, but its as I say we packed all our things up and the order for going was cancelled, and then we came the next morning, and the mucking about made my head ache!

We got in Withernsea about 6 O'clock. And if you will I want about 5 shillings sent me - Dont forget to register it, it might get lost.

Seventy from our company from Cowden are up here with us.

Well I expect you would like to know where we are sleeping. Well I have still got my pal with me and we sleep on boards in a room all to ourselves, and its a big house nearly facing the sea. I am getting plenty of sea-side sort of thing.

Well dear Mother I cannot say when I am coming to see you, but I expect we shall all be having 5 days soon, so cheer up and keep on smiling.

Write soon, hoping Dad is better by now. We have amile each way to walk for our meals. Hoping all are in the pink,

From your loving son,

CYRIL

For "K". xxxxxxxxxxxxxxxxxxxxxxxxxx

253294. Withernsea.   Dec 19th 1916.

Dear Lillian

Well I have received the parcel and I must thank Mother and Dad for the watch, its just what I wanted and I went on patrol last night and I thought the Cowden patrol was bad enough but its not a patch on it over here. I done guards here, but we are doing the lot as another company was doing patrols before.

I was putting Young St on my letter, but just put what you see on the top as we are given the letters at the dining place.

I had a parcel from Auntie Alice and it has been stopping at Cowden, but pleased to say that I have received it- - also I received the five shillings today.

It is better to register money letters now as "A" company is a thousand strong and they may get stolen.

The parcel was four days late from Worcester, and Richard sent me one that was also four days late owing to, stopping at Cowden. Its very good of Richard, sending me a parcel, also his mother sent me a birthday card.

Well, Mother tell Dad I guest it was as watch. I am in the rotten Reg again and the pack enough to kill us. We have a hundred and twenty rounds to carry and our guns.

Tell Theo to keep his job he would not like to be one of us.

I have found the way to wind it up. Its very useful present. I could not have wished for a better thing, but should have liked to have had a birthday in a different place as you know (home).

Well, Lillian You see I was moved too quick to get you those things from Hornsea, but never mind waite later.

The garrison battalian men dont get a Christmas pass according to the regulations, they read to us over here, but I am now in a service battallian I might stand a chance.

I am longing to see your faces again, absence makes the heart grow fonder - I have found that out.

Thank you for the chok its extra, and the other sweets. I expect you will be pleased to know we get plenty of food and thats half the battle, and we also get plenty of marching about and cleaning. I was cleaning my brasses on my equipment from 12am till 7 O'clock on Sunday night. Not bad is it.?

For the first day or so we have a mile to walk there and back every meal, and Friday we go for our meals with full marching order - - I am writing this letter to all of you - - - - -

(Unfinished.)

25

Cyril's Father
Theo Morrell

Cyril's Mother
Sarah Ellen

Kathleen, Cyril's sister

Theo, Cyril's brother

Leslie, Cyril's brother

Lillian, Cyril's sister

Auntie Elsie

Auntie Alice

William (Billy) Morrell who emigrated to Australia

NOTICE PAPER to be sent to each man who has been attested and transferred to the Army Reserve under the provisions of the Royal Warrant of the 20th October, 1915

[This Notice Paper should be despatched so that it will reach the addressee at least 14 clear days before he is required to present himself at the appointed place.

In accordance with the provisions of Section 24 (1) of the Reserve Forces Act, 1882, "evidence of the delivery at the last registered place of abode of a man belonging to the Army Reserve of a notice, or of a letter addressed to such man, and containing a notice, shall be evidence that such notice was brought to the knowledge of such man.")

Surname *Morrell*

Christian Name *Thos Cyril*

Address *1 Cemetery Rd*
Bilston

Number as shown on the Card, Army Form W. 3194 .... *5*

Group Number *4*

You are hereby warned that you will be required to rejoin for service with the Colours on the **28 MAY 1916** 191

You should therefore present yourself at *DRILL HALL, BILSTON*

on the above date, not later than *2-30* o'clock, bringing this paper with you.

This will be struck out if the man resides within a mile of the place at which he is required to present himself

~~A Railway Warrant is enclosed herewith.~~

R dento Signature.

15/5/16 Date.

DRILL HALL, BILSTON. Place.

Rank.

Appointment.

N.B.—Particular attention is called to Section 15 of the Reserve Forces Act, 1882, which provides that where a man belonging to the Army Reserve is called out on Permanent service, and such man, without leave lawfully granted or such sickness or other reasonable excuse as may be allowed in the prescribed manner, fails to appear at any time and place at which he is required on such calling out to attend, he shall be guilty, according to the circumstances, of deserting, within the meaning of Section 12, or of absenting himself without leave within the meaning of Section 15 of the Army Act, 1881.

(23675) Wt.19273—M 412. 250,000. 2/16. S. P. & Co., Ltd. Forms/W.3195/2.

Cyril's Call Up Papers

(4 22 33) W410⸗—8103 10,000 7/16 HWV(7P1809/3⸗ G16/9⸗4
6698—8901 20,000 9/16

Form D.

Any further letter on this subject should be addressed to—

The Secretary,
War Office,
Alexandra House,
Kingsway,
London, W.C.2
and the number below quoted.

C. 2. Casualties.

No. *392645*.

WAR OFFICE,

LONDON, S.W.,

27th March 1917.

25394 Private J. C. Howell, 10th East Yorkshire Regiment.

Madam.

In reply to ~~your~~ *an* enquiry, *on your behalf* of the *21st March 1917.*

I am commanded by the Army Council to inform you that the soldier named above has been reported in a casualty list which has reached this office as having *died of wounds on the 12th March 1917.*

I am to express the sympathy of the Army Council with the soldier's relatives.

Every endeavour is being made with a view to the early collection of the personal effects of the deceased, and of the amount due to the estate, but some delay must necessarily occur.

I am, *Madam.*

Your obedient Servant,

B.B. Brade

*Mrs J. Howell.
1 Cemetery Road.
Dilston.
Staffordshire.*

Notification of Cyril's death

36

WAR GRAVES
PHOTOGRAPH AND WREATH COMPANY
W. A. PROSSER (Secretary)
ALBERT (Somme)

France

Established — 1920

EMPLOYING ONLY BRITISH EX-SERVICE MEN WHO LIVE IN FRANCE

Dear sir or Madam,

Please find enclosed the photograhs which you kindly ordered
from this association, and which we trust are to your satisfaction.

After you have examined same, we shall be pleased to receive
your remittance (in the special enveloppe enclosed, and which MUST
BE REGISTERED) and at your earliest convenience.

The Cemetery in which your relative Lies is
Sucrerie Plot *1* Row *I* N° *11*

The amount due is *3* photographs

Wreath *11/-*

Postage *6*

Total . . . *11/6*

Extra copies 2/ each, remittance for same should accompany
this order,

Thanking you, and assuring you of our complete obedience to
your orders.

Yours faithfully.

W. A. PROSSER, Sec

W. G. P. — W. Co

P. S. — *Special enlargement of this Photograh, mesuring 50 x 40, cm. can be obtained for the sum of 12/6 each.*

Charges made for photographs of Cyril's grave

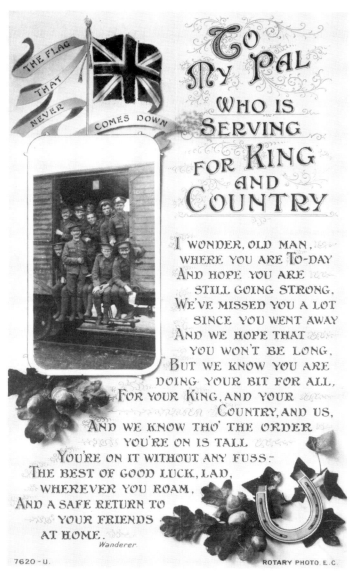

Postcard sent to Cyril from his friend Richard

St Leonard's Church School
Lillian as pupil/teacher standing left

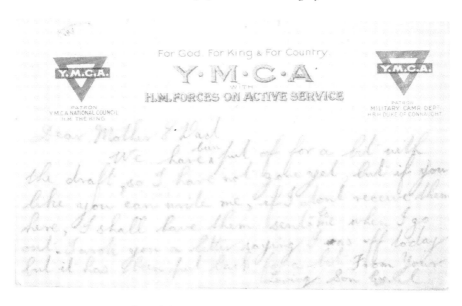

One of the postcards sent home from Cyril

Director of Graves Registration & Enquiries.

Begs to forward as requested a Photograph of
the Grave of :—

Name ___Morrell___

Rank and Initials ___Pte. T. C.___

Regiment ___10 East Yorkshire Regt.___

Position of Grave ___Queen's Military Cemetery, Colincamps___

Nearest Railway Station ___Wailly Wailly Wailloy.___

All communications respecting this Photograph should quote
the number (___17109.3___) and be addressed to :—

Director of Graves Registration and Enquiries,

War Office,

Winchester House,

St. James's Square,

London, S.W., 1.

Owing to the circumstances in which the photographic work is carried
on, the Director regrets that in some cases only rough Photographs can
be obtained.

"Cyril's" durable wooden cross"

40

Withernsea. Bat 3

Dec 25th 1916.

Dear Mother and Dad,

Just to thank you all for the parcel, you may of thought I had not received it - but yes I got it allright.

Well we had for breakfast liver and bacon and tomatoes, for dinner we had roast beef, sprouts and ginger beer and an apple - we also have another treat for tea, so we have not done so bad after all.

It would have gone down better if I had been at home. I have forgotten to tell you -- we had plump-pudden and sorce for dinner.

Well, did you receive my Christmas card? I heard from Mr J H Holden the other day for a wonder.

The cake is extra that you sent me. I thank you very much for the parcel. Tell Lillian that Harold wants to know where my little sister is hiding herself as he would like to see her - God bless her.

I hope Dad is himself again, tell him to keep on smiling - the war wont last very long now. I am trying hard for a pass so dont be surprized to see me at any time.

Tell Kathleen that I say there is no girls in Withernsea like her. I have not seen one like her yet.

Well I have enjoyed myself pretty fare considering, but I hope to be with you next year - not in the army no thank you.

I got up at 6am this morning and I was helping a chum to clean out the Y M C A , so I began feasting before breakfast and have not stopped yet so thats one good thing, that we all have plenty to eat.

Well Dear Mother and Dad, I must close now as it is nearly tea-time and of-course I cant miss that at any cost so, so long.

Hoping all have had a good time and that all are in the pink as it leaves me at present. From your loving son,

CYRIL.

For "K". xxxxxxxxxxxx

Excuse the scribble, as I am in a hurry.

Withernsea.   Dec 30th 1916.

Dear Lillian,

Well I got the parcel allright and tell Kathleen that her brother is delighted with the scarf and I am delighted to hear that she is getting on so well. I shall hardly believe she is getting on so quick if I dont come over soon and see her.

Well you know all day Christmas and Saturdays and Sundays it is all alike here. We do drills just the same as week-days - not a minute for anythink - only clean up for the next days parade. We finish at four thirty pm and as soon as we fall out we have got to fall in again for tea or dinner such as the case may be, its a lot worse than when we came away the first time.

Well Lillian I expect we shall be going to South Doulton for our course and after that means a draught pass before going out to France.

Dont tell Mar, she will go mad, but is has got to be done.

Yes I had plenty of cigs this time. Of course I do have a few left now but they will soon go when you have plenty of pals.

There is one thing I have to tell you and that is all Christmas passes are stopped at this place, but if I had been at Cowden I should have got one - but you see how they have all of us trapped.

If ever we were to have another war I watch I went accross the herring pond before they caught me napping (Only draught passes are allowed- - the rotten dogs.)

I went to a concert twice last week and we had a good time. We had refreshments passed round and fags etc. Well it was very good for nothink, but we were up till 12 O'clock pm cleaning and last to be up in the morning. The same time we had a card each which I have put in the envelope. On Friday we went for a route march - about 12 miles and done drill in the morning part. Well after that we came back soaked to the skin but I had another change for one good thing and then had to patrol the cliff all night - so thats the way we are being served and we are to be cleaned up the next morning to do our duty just the same.

Yes Sister, I feel older I can tell you, and every young lad the same as me are worried to death without anythink else.

If I come over I shall go to Worcester for a day to see them all, but just to break the new to Mar - you know if she wants - - -

(Incomplete)

42

Withernsea

Dear Dad,

I expect you think it is time I wrote you. Well Dad it struck me last night in bed about the dog lisence and I can trust you for seeing that it is payed. Tell mar to give it to you out of my money and then Theo or Lillian can get it. I expect they will be on to those sort of things this time sharp.

Well we are going through it here again. I shall be glad when I am going to France. We are on from 6 O'clock in a morning till seven at night. without having 5 mins rest, only time to eat our meals. The people do go on about it here - the way they rush us.

When we go to dig trenches we go full marching order and sometimes we go full marching order for our meals, all our commrades are fed-up with it.

Fancy having a kit inspection last night, and it lasted two hours in our own time, even hairs were looked at and if they wanted cutting they had to stop over and have it done. It was getting on for 11 o'clock before we got into bed and we have to be up at half past five.

Talk about the army wants men, that rubbish, they want steam-engines not men.

Well I expect you will have guessed that when I come home it will be my draught pass before going out. You see we are entitled to a X-Mas leave - but they wont give it to us, and also they have stopped even week-ends. If the Germans are treated any worse than us then God help them.

You should see my hair, they have cut it like a convict and the rule is you have to have it done every three weeks whether it wants cutting or not. I only have about three long hairs at the front so you can gess what its like. Well Dad you may think that I grumble but its only too true, every word that I have wrote, but never mind, if I get out of this I shall go accross the water as soone as I hear that we are going to have another war again, for I might just as well be thousands of miles away from home as be here for what passes are allowed.

Well Dad, I must close. Hoping to see you all soone. I send my best wishes to all. wishing all a happy new year and I hope all are in the pink as it leaves me.

Tell Theo, to keep his job and stick to it for all his worth.

Your loving son,

CYRIL.
"K" xxxxxxxxxxxxxxxxxxxxxxxxxxxxxxxxxxx

NB Cyril's concern regarding a dog licence was due to the fact that he purchased the dog (a large Irish Wolf Hound) to protect his mother and sisters during his stay in the army as his father and brothers had often to work lake into the night leaving the women alone, and the family house backed on to a large desolate meadow which was frequently occupied by troublesome gypsies.

Unfortunately the dog proved to be too vicious towards anyone other than family and after seriously injuring a lady caller, (who's private nursing was subsequently paid for by my grand-parents), the dog eventually had to be shot by a local police officer as regretfully requested by my grandfather.

Cyril was told that the dog was to be sold.

Withernsea.

Dear Mother,

Well I received Lillians letter today Saturday, and I was surprized to hear about Leslie losing his job, he wants to keep a job at this time for if he ever gets in the army he will repent the day he joined.

You are having company then, how is she getting on with Kathleen. I heard that Uncle Hal is in bed, I am sorry to hear that, but if he was in the army he would have to be near Deaths door before he could go to bed. So I advise him to, keep away. What do you say??

Well those shirts I sent home, I will get you to alter the sleeves and wash them out. Get them done as quick as possible and I can bring them back when I come over, and it wont be so long - so please get them done.

Well about the dog, dont pay the lisence if you are going to sell it it will do for me what you do about him.

Well I must close, hoping all are in the pink. From your loving son,

CYRIL.

For Kathleen. xxxxxxxxxxxxxxxxxxxxx

(South Doulton ? ?)   Jan 10th 1917.

Dear Lillian,

I expect you think I have forgotten you but I said in my last letter I was about to fire my course.

Well we got here on Monday and was wet to the skin, it rained and hailed all day. Well there are about thirty of us here from Withernsea and we are going on very nicely. Today I have already made ninety points with shooting and we have only got to fire another 25 rounds, so you can expect to see me on Monday.

Well I did not finish telling you about getting wet. Well we had to dry our clothes by a big stove and we did not do any parades that day. Well the rain kept on all day the next day so we only had rifle practice that day in our hut. We are having a better time, but it will only last till Friday, so that is the reason I have not put my address at the top. But write me to my own address if you write me and I shall get it when I go back.

The weather today has been frosty and I hope it will keep like it till we return to Withernsea as the walk from the camp to the railway station is two miles and the same distance to the firing range.

This place must be a lovely spot in the summer, but its no-mans land now this weather is on.

There are about 100 big huts and a Y M turned or made out of a hut, and a big church in the distance and thats how far as I have been.

We have to parade at eight thirty in a morning - not so bad is it ? But I get up in a morning the same time as Withernsea, but you see we have got plenty of time to clean ourselves up.

Well I dont think I can tell you much more news at this time, only we are firing tomorrow with gas helmets over our heads - that is to stop the gas as the Germans will send if I go out.

If I get another 30 points tomorrow I am entitled to wear cross-guns!

I must close, hoping all are in the pink as it leaves me, only for my bad teeth but I am thinking of having two out when I get home.

Well so long from your loving brother,

CYRIL.

Give these to Kathleen. xxxxxxxxxxxxxxxxxxxxxxxxxxxxxxxxxxxx
                        xxxxxxxx
                        xxx

Withernsea.   Jan 13th 1917.

Dear Dad,

I received a letter from you last night dated from 1st January. I dont know whether you made a mistake in the date but I got it and so I dont care.

Well Dad I have come back to Withernsea once more and we have had some funny weather while we have been away. We were freezing on Thursday while the snow lay deep on the hills. It seemed a funny world to me that day. I never went out of the camp as it was so bad.

I have made a hundred and twenty five pounds - not so bad is it?

Well tell Kathleen that her Cyril is coming on Tuesday and I expect it will be about four O'clock before I get home at the earliest.

Well you should see my letters this week that I have to answer back - you see they are letters saved for me while I have been away.

I had a letter from Mrs Pye from Worcester, so you see I have plenty writing me and it keeps me busy.

Well I must close now hoping you and all at home are in the best of health as it leaves me at present,

From your loving son,

CYRIL.

For Kathleen. xxxxxxxxxxxxxxxxxxxxxxxxxxxxxx

When is it her birthday. I have forgotten the date - Thank Mother for doing that little job I asked her.

So long.

Pte T C Morrell 25394
Comp A Batt 3 E Yorks
Withernsea.

Jan 21st 1917.

Dear Mother and father,

I got in about 1 O'clock and we had a very nice nights rest - - I dont think!
It was too late to get our blankets so we had to lay down as we were. I
was not the only one, the pals who stop in my room. We left one another
and I never saw them till I got to the house, so you see I had the journey
all on my own and today Sunday, we have been on parade till six O'clock
and you may gess we have had very little time to write. So if the letter
sounds out of place you will have to excuse me.
Well I have not wrote to Auntie Alice yet, but that seems to worry me, not
going to see them.
I hope you are not down-hearted for me, I shall soone be home again, and
I felt down for a bit - but never mind it wont last for ever.
I thought about all of you and thought there was a change to when I left
you first, but dont worry for you and Dad looked older, and when I come
home again I want to see you both look younger.
Well God bless you all and remember me to Grandma, hoping all are in
the pink as it leaves me at present, from your loving son,

CYRIL.

For Kathleen - God bless her. xxxxxxxxxxxxxxxxxxxx

Withernsea.   Jan 27th 1917.

Dear Sister,

I dont think I have heard from home since I got back, I am not shure but
my word we have gone through it again. On Friday, that was yesterday
we went 16 miles on a route march and I might say my feet are very sore
and my draft boots rub me, that is the reason.
Well sister I have heard that we go to France tomorrow night, we start
about five O'clock. So look out for me passing through Bilston.
Just try and break the news quiet at home as I say, because I know it will
upset them all at home. We have a bit more training at the base so thats
one good job.
Well I must close now - hoping all are in the pink as it leaves me only for
my feet,
From your loving brother,

                              CYRIL.

              For Kathleen. xxxxxxxxxxxxxxxxxxxxxxxxxxxxxxxx

Y M C A Post Card.
Withernsea

29th Jan 1917.

Dear Mother and Dad,

We have been put off for a bit with the draft, so I have not gone yet, but if you like you can write me. If I dont receive them here I shall have them sent to me when I go out.
I wrote you a letter saying I was off today, but is has been put back for a bit,

From your loving son,

CYRIL.

On active service
S C A camp to Home

Feb 2nd 1917.

Dear Mother and Father,

I expect you think that I had forgotten you. Well I have been moving, and I have been going on pretty fare. We are under canvers, and I might say it is COLD.

If you have sent me a letter I daresay it will come allright. Tell Dad to get those boots healed and laped and they will make him an extra pair for the summer.

Let me have a newspaper every week while I am in this camp. We cant buy any here. Well I dont know anythink else to tell you about this time - - I am only writing to let you know that I am still alive and kicking - - My address on the other side.

Wishing you all the best of luck, from your loving son,

CYRIL.

For Kathleen (Cheer up.) xxxxxxxxxxxxxxxxxxxxxxxxxxxxxxx

(Over)

Pte C T Morrell
25394
6 Batt E York
371 B W S17A Po
B E F,
France.

Feb 10th 1917.

France.

Dear Sister,

I expect by now you have received my letters. Well we have been moved again so please take notice of the address, this is my proper address now;

> Pte T C Morrell 25394
> 10 Batt,
> B Camp, 7 Platt
> E York.
> B E F France.

Well I am going on pretty fare, but I have a cold, send me somethink for it will you? I have not heard from you yet, also send me on the paper every week. I cant tell you any think about were we are, but keep on smiling and we shall soon be back at Blighty.

How is my little Kathleen going on? I am always thinking about her. I have not got much news to tell you but when you write I want you to tell me all the news you can. Have you heard from Billy Morrell yet? How are you all at home? I may say that its Feb again, - its so funny what happens every year at this time - - let me see the end of this month, what do you say ?.

Well I must close now, hoping all are in good health as it leaves me only for a cold, from,

Your loving brother,

CYRIL.

For Kathleen. xxxxxxxxxxxxxxxxxxxxx

Church Army Recreation Hut   Feb 13th 1917.
On Active Service
With the British Expeditionary Force.

Dear Mother and Dad,

Let me have a letter as soon as you can. I hope you will get the one that I sent you before this one. Will you let Auntie Elsie know that I am in France, I expect she will think that it is unkind of me not to answer the last letter that they sent.

Well I am going on allright so far, but I may say it is very cold. Let me know how you are going on at home, and can you make anythink out about the boots yet? Keep on gessing and let Lillian see it and she might drop to it.

It is Saturday today, and its all the same to us, the week days are.

I am going to write Auntie Alice after I have done this.

We sleep in a tent and put our blankets all down together and that's the only thing to do to keep warm at nights.

Well I must close, hoping all are in the pink as it leaves me at present,

From your loving son,

CYRIL.

For Kathleen. xxxxxxxxxxxxxxxxxxxxx

(God bless you all.)

France.

My Dear Sister,

Thanks for the letters dated 7th and 31st. I was delighted to hear from you. Well when the letter was given to me I could hardly eat my tea, so you see how it is to have a letter from home.

Very sorry to hear that Dad has been bad, I do hope he will be himself again soon. I expect its working over and trouble thats upsetting him. I have only received those two letters so far, but you can send me a parcel now any time. You have my latest address and it will be allright. Thank Kathleen for the little girls she sent me, tell her they are all well in health and they are a long way a way.

I wrote Uncle Hal about four days back, I was very anxious to, know how he was, and the letter quite relieved me when it came as I had a funny dream.

The wallet will be very nice, Its what I want very bad, and a little money - we are drawing 5 franks a week. I am getting into the new money you waite and I'll come and talk french to you.

I wrote to Auntie alice asking her to tell you to send some toothache jelly from Shelleys, also I would like Auntie Fanny's address. Auntie Alice said that she was knitting a pair for me. Its very kind of her.

Fancy Neil with his woman, its a little strange for Neil taking upon himself, Ah!

Yes its very cold here, but we still keep on doing it.

Well we get one or two 'friends' on our shirts, but thats nothink, so long as they are not Germans, What do you say ?

Well I think I have said all this time, hoping all are in the pink by now, I must close now, with love to all the dear folks at home,

From your loving brother,

CYRIL.

For Kathleen. xxxxxxxxxxxxxxxxxxxxxxxxxxxxxxx

P.S. Dont forget to tell the boys at home I have not forgot them.
I do hope Leslie is behaving himself towards you.

France. (Location withheld.)   Feb 19th 1917.

Dear Mother and Dad,

Your letter to hand written on the tenth. Well I am still struggling along.
Well the weather it is rotten.
I had a letter from Mr Page - I was surprized to hear from them so soon
saying they were sending me a parcel, so I am expecting it. I will write to
them soon.
We have been moving again, so I expect this letter will be behind, so dont
worry about that.
I cannot tell you much news now as you know they are strict.
Well Dad fags are very cheap out here, it does not pay you to buy them in
England, so I would sooner have the money.
Thanks for sending me a wallet it will come in so useful, I could also do
with some writing paper and envelopes as this is what I have carried with
me from old England.
Dont send me Oxo clubes, send me cocoa tablets or coffie and sweets with
pepermint in them.
Yes Lillian did say that Harold was a Sunday school teacher, she tolled me
in the last letter.
Well I am sure the parcel will come in very handy, you know we look for
a parcel like a child looking for a doll.
You have heard from Willy then at last. Poor old Billy, Dad you dont
know what a soldier goes through - it looks very nice on pictures dont it?
Well never mind, I hope God will put his mighty hand down soon, either
for worse - which I feel shure it will be for the best.
Well I dont know any more news this time to tell you. Hoping all are in
good spirit and health as it leaves me at present, from your loving son,

             CYRIL.

                        For "K" God bless her. xxxxxxxxxxxxxxxxx

P S. I hope Leslie is a good lad and that everythink is sailing along
smooth at home.

France. (Location withheld.)

Dear Mother and Father,

I am quite allright at present, but I have not received a parcel yet - Have you sent one to the base. I expect you have not yet received my last letter - have you because my address was on it and we are not allowed to send it every time we write.

Well it is Pte T C Morrell 25394, B Camp, 10 E. Yorks, 7 Platt. (And dont lose it this time.)

Mr Page wrote me saying there was a parcel coming for me - but I have not received that, you might tell him will you ?

How are you all getting on at home, you will write often will you?

I am always thinking about you as you are about me. I expect you will think that I have forgotten you, but dont worry because we have to write when we can. I daresay you know my circumstances.

How is my little sister going on ?

Well I am expecting somethink I can tell you. I might tell you I get a Rum ration and we all need it what we go through.

I have received your papers you sent me, thank you very much, its quite a change to read an English paper.

Well I hope everyone is allright at home. I will write has you know when I have time. I must close now, hoping Leslie and Theo is allright. Tell them to write me, they have more time than me and I should be delighted to have a line from them, I must close, hoping all are in the pink, has it leaves me at present, From your loving son,

CYRIL.   Write soon.

I have just received your letter today dated Feb 23rd, but have not had a parcel yet either from you or from the Chapel. Yes I have seen some Germans, I have seen more than I wanted to.

We have had a bath and we wanted one I can tell you.

I wrote Auntie Elsie some time back. If she has not received it yet it got lost. I will write them again soone.

You tell Victor Lett he is better off where he is.

I have seen more than I expected to. I have been in mud and water up to my waist, so you can gess how the trenches are - but keep on smiling till the boys come home.

God bless you all.

For Kathleen. xxxxxxxxxxxxxxxxxxxxxxxxxxxx

March 6th 1917.

Dear Father,

Thanks for your kind letter. I received it on the 5th.
Mother asked me last time if I wanted some candles, Yes. I have plenty of soap. I do hope I shall receive the other parcels they cost such a lot to get lost. Have you addressed it to the base or where did you address it to.
Well as you know we are always ready to eat our meals and a parcel comes in handy.
Yes I expect they are short of men in my trade, and we have had some frost, we get it over here just the same.
I have not come across Niel or Willie yet, in fact I have not seen anyone yet as I know, We have to make chums with anyone.
Well I am pretty fare so far, but its very cold and we have to do our best to get warm. Its not like the old home where you have a nice fire and a bed to go to at night when you have finished work.
Yes, we get plenty of stew, but it goes down like a bit of duck - I have not had any frog yet nor dont want any.
You see I have very little time to write, so you may tell Lillian I have not forgotten her.
Well Dad how do you think the war is going on? We can only see as far as our nose - I hope it wont be long what do you say ?
Thank Kathleen for the kisses, God bless her, and I hope you are not worrying about me, I am going on allright.
If the post is a bit late dont worry and sometimes letters get lost. I sent Auntie Alice a letter and she said she had not received it by your last letter, so you see they dont always get to their destinations.
I must close now, hoping all are in the best of health as it leaves me at present.

From your loving son,

CYRIL.

for Kathleen. xxxxxxxxxxxxxxxxxxxxxxxx

57

March 9th 1917.

LETTER TO SISTER WHEN ON ACTIVE SERVICE PRINTED ON OFFICIAL ENVELOPE:-

Note - correspondence in this envelope need not be censored regimentally.
The contents are liable to examination at the Base.
The following certificate must be signed by the writer:-

I CERTIFY ON MY HONOUR THAT THE CONTENTS OF THIS ENVELOPE REFER TO NOTHING BUT PRIVATE AND FAMILY MATTERS.

     Signature. (Name only) T C MORRELL.

Dear Sister,
You must excuse me not writing to you but when I send a letter home it is for all of you.
I am sorry to say that the letter got burnt with that address you sent me of Auntie Fanny, so, the next letter you send me please write it down again.
I have also been wondering if they would allow me to send my address as they are so strict.
I am in want of a pipe we get plenty of tobacco and not many fags - get a cheap one.
Well we are not in tents or huts as you can partly gess, we are down in the mine Dad.
Remember me to Vaney, Prouds Lane - Dont let our kid know!
You know it takes me all my time to write home and one or two more places - but home first.
Yes, I expect the place are looking empty, so many young men coming out. I wish I could drop on someone as I knew. I might drop on someone yet. AH!
Well Sister I must close now, with best of luck. Hoping all are in the best of health as it leaves me at present,
From your loving brother,

       CYRIL.

    For Kathleen. xxxxxxxxxxxxxxxxxxxxxxxx

March 15th 1917.

From. Pte Nash.
France.

Dear Madam,

Enclosed find pocket wallet which arrived here on March 13th for your son Cyril.

I am sorry to inform you that he was wounded on the 12th and died shortly afterwards.

He was my friend shortly after being called up and we have been together since.

I can but express my deepest sympathy and sorrow to you and your family in the loss of your son.

I beg to remain yours truly,

Pte A Nash. 25360.

France.
Pte Nash.

Dear Mrs Morrell,
just a few lines in answer to your letter of the 12th.
I am glad to say that I am keeping quite well and hope that you and all
your family are the same.
I am in the same platoon that Cyril was in and we were mates together.
The officer you say censors our letters was in charge of our platoon.
With regard to what things he had on him, I cannot say what has become
of them, but I have forwarded you his woollen scarf which was the only
thing that I got belonging to him and that he had left in the dug-out.
I have received two letters from you previous to this and have answered
them both, also all the questions that it has been possible for me to
answer, but I noticed that according to Pte Cox's letters that you had not
received them so I told him to answer all your questions that you had
asked me to tell you.
I am sorry to say that he died while the doctor was dressing his wounds.
His wounds were in the side.
I cannot say whether he was buried in a cemetry or not, but I know the
name of the place where he was buried, but I cannot tell you the name.
He was conscious till the end and according to what I have been told his
only cry was for his mother.
I may say that I do smoke.
I think this is all that I know at present, but will do my best to get further
information for you and will let you know as soon as possible.

Yours,

Pte A Nash.

May 31st 1917.

France.
From Pte W Moran 36327.

Dear Mrs Morrell,

having been informed by Pte Nash you are making inquiries about your gallant son Cyril Morrell, who joined this battalion with others on or about the 4th Feb.

Well, Dear Mrs Morrell, I am the only one left out of the party that was with your son at the time.

It was about three hours before we were relived that an order came for water to be taken to company HQ. Myself and four more men were told to go with it. Your son was one of them.

Well we went with the water and as we came back a shell exploded in the middle of us.

Myself and Pte Westerby was the nearest to the shell when it exploded. We heard it coming and I shouted,

"Get down lads" We all got down - I was first to recover - The sight I shall never forget, I asked,

"Are you all hit?". And someone shouted,

"I am Paddy". (Paddy is my name in the Batt.)
I got him up into my arms, it was your son Cyril, he said,

"Dont leave me Paddy"
I said   "Cheer up lad you are alright for Blighty"
I got the others into the trench - all of them, one poor lad was killed on the spot. I then got the doctor and stretcher bearers on the job and they were soon all bandaged up and I carried them to the dressing station. But I am very sorry to say your son died on the way.

But cheer up and Almighty God will look after your gallant son in Heaven I hope.

Well Mrs Morrell, I went to bury your son myself the next day, but the division that relieved us had already done so.

However, I went to his grave-side to make sure it was him and I read the card on his grave, yes, it was him.

He is buried in the Sucerie cemetery, near a village called Hebuterne, where more of our gallant lads are laid.

There will be a cross now to mark the place where your gallant son is laid at rest.

So I have told you all that happened on that fatal night. It was a sad sight for those that saw me carrying those poor lads into that trench. They now call me "Paddy" or "The man who lived to tell the tale".

Dear friend, I have had my share of this war, I was in the battle of Ypres and the battle of the Somme.

I returned to dear old England in Feb 1915, with shell-shock, and I came out here again in December 1916, and I have been over the top twice during the time I have been in France this time - so I think I have done my bit, but I always pray to Almighty God to bring me safely through and he has answered my prayers.

I have two children to live for and I wish it was all over.

So now Dear Mrs Morrell, I must draw to a close, hoping my letter will set your mind at rest, and I will always welcome a letter from anyone in old England.

Hoping you are all keeping well at home and allow me to remain one of the boys that is helping to keep the old flag flying.

W Moran 36327.

FORM D.
WAR OFFICE
London SW.
27th March 1917.

"C"2 Casualties.
No 392645.

25394. Pte T C Morrell.
10th East Yorkshire Regiment.

Madam,

In reply to an enquiry on your behalf of the 21st March 1917. I am commanded by the Army Council to inform you that the soldier named above has been reported in a casualty list which has reached this office as having died of wounds on 12th March 1917.

I am to express the sympathy of the Army Council with the soldier's relatives.

Every endeavour is being made with a view to the early collection of the personal effects of the deceased, and of the amount due to the estate, but some delay must neccessarily occur.

I am, Madam,

Your obedient Servant,

Mrs T Morrell.
1, Cemetery Rd
Bilston
Staffs.

FORM E
WAR OFFICE.
6th June 1917

Dear Madam,

In replying to your enquiry of 6th April 1917, I have to say that Pte T C Morrell is buried in the Sucrerie Military cemetery, Colincamps, North of Albert.
The grave has been registered in this office, and is marked by a durable wooden cross with an inscription bearing his name, rank, and regiment and the date of his death.

Yours faithfully,

Captain
Staff Captain.
For Brig General.

To Mrs T Morrell
1 Cemetery Rd
Bilston
Staffs

FORM C
WAR OFFICE.
4th July 1917

Dear Madam,

In reply to your letter of 17 6 17, I have to say that your request for a photograph of the grave of Pte T C Morrell has been noted.
There will be some unavoidable delay owing to the difficulty, which you will easily understand of carrying on photographic work at the front, but a copy of the photograph will be sent to you as soon as circumstances permit owing to military activity at the present time, it has been neccessary to suspend temporarily photographic work in certain areas at the front.

Yours faithfully,

Staff Captain,
For Brig General.

1 Cemetery Rd
Bilston

France 643.

entry in "The WAR GRAVES of the BRITISH EMPIRE"

Sucrerie Military Cemetery,

Colincamps

France.

Plot 1   Row 1   No 11.

Compiled and published by order of the Imperial War Graves Commission London. 1929. (EST 1920).

MORRELL. Pte Thomas Cyril 25394 10th Bn East Yorkshire Regt.
Died of wounds 12th March 1917 aged 23. Son of Theophilus and Sarah Ellen Morrell of Avondale, 110, Wellington Rd, Bilston Staffs.

I. I. 11.

SUCRERIE MILITARY CEMETERY.
COLINCAMPS.

Cemetery Index No Fr 643.

Colincamps is a village and commune in the Department of the Somme, seven miles North of Albert, and the Sucrerie Military Cemetery is a mile East of the village, 300 yards North of the road from Mailly-Maillet to Serre.

It stands on the South side of a private avenue leading from Colincamps to the side of Sucrerie, (or sugar-beet factory) de Mailly-Maillet; but is approached from the other side by a path. The nearest railway station is at Mailly-Maillet, a mile to the South-West on the light railway from Albert to Doullens.

The cemetery was begun by French troops in the early summer of 1915, and extended to the West by British units from July in that year - until - with intervals - December 1918. It was called at first the 10th Brigade Cemetery. Until the German retreat in March 1917, it was rather more than a mile from the front line; and from the end of March 1918 (when the New Zealand Division was engaged at fighting at the Sucrerie) to the following August it was under fire.

The 285 French and twelve German graves were removed to other cemeteries after the Armistice, and in consequence there are gaps in the lettering of the rows.

The Cemetery now contains the graves of 827 soldiers from the United Kingdon, 65 from New Zealand and two from Canada. The un-named graves are 74 in number and special memorials are erected to seven soldiers from the United Kingdom, known or believed to be buried among them.

The area is 7562 square yards; it is enclosed by a low brick wall and planted with Limes and Cherry trees. The cemetery stands on a wide plateau among corn-fields.

(Imperial War Graves Commission, London 1929.)

THE MORRELL FAMILY

The Morrell family became residents of Bilston when in 1827 Jabez Morrell moved from Handsworth to Bilston to marry his young wife Maria.

They had several children, although many of them died in early infancy. Their son Theophillus, born in 1830, went on to become a shrewd businessman and earned his living as a local auctioneer and pawn-broker. He and his wife Sarah had three sons, William, Cornellius and Theophillus, the latter being the father of Thomas Cyril - the writer of the letters.

Theophillus Morrell
Born August 1864.

Theo and his brother William (Billy) were partners in the firm Morrell Brothers, Builders of Bilston. Their yard sited close by the land where once the old market stood.

Apart from building several residences in the parish they were also involved in the building of the old market hall and the early Bilston baths. Although a thriving business, Theophillus found it a struggle to survive for a time when his brother Billy left Bilston without prior notice and emigrated to Australia taking most of the firm's funds along with him.

For the first part of his married life Theo lived with his wife Sarah Ellen (Nellie), in Princess St before moving to Stowheath Lane and then later into No.1 Cemetery Road, Bilston.

After the tragic death of their son Cyril, Theo and the family moved to 110 Wellington Road, a house which Theo had formerly helped to build. This final move was considered necessary as the view over-looking the graveyard from Cemetery Road caused much grief to Nellie due to her recent bereavement.

They remained in this house until their deaths, Theo in 1946 aged 81 years and Nellie in November 1951 aged 82 years.

Their eldest daughter Lillian lived alone from then on in the family house until her death in 1985 at the age of 92 years. Throughout all this time she kept Cyril's letters safely in his 'box'.

Sarah Ellen Morrell (Nee Hill)
Born March 18th 1869.

The eldest daughter of Thomas and Sarah. She married Theo on September 30th 1891 at Salam Baptist Chapel, Wood St, Bilston.

Sarah Ellen was always known as 'Nellie'. She had a brother Harry who eventually moved to Worcester where he ran a drapery business and three younger sisters, Alice, Mary and Elsie, who were to be the aunties refered to in Cyril's letters.

Sadly Nellie's father died at the age of 41 and as the oldest member of the family she took on a lot of the family responsibilities for the sake of her mother, and even after her marriage to Theo, with his help she managed to ensure that her mother coped financially and otherwise through difficult times.

She was a devoted mother, and having lost one son at an early age due to meningitis, she was particularly protective towards her other children. The thought of Cyril being in the army caused her much distress, especially so, when he received his orders to go to France.

On Cyril's last leave before his journey to the front, Nellie held a farewell party for her beloved son. She was a supersitious lady and was dismayed when she realised that thirteen people were sitting down to dine together, fearing that such an unlucky number would surely mean that she would never see her son again!

Lillian May Morrell. Sister to Cyril.

Born June 27th 1892.

Lillian had a twin brother, Cornellius, who died from meningitis at the age of 2 years 8 months.

Lillian was the strongest member of the Morrell household, and perhaps the person who Cyril chose to confide in most, depending on her to alleviate his mother's fears for his safety - she was the recipient of many of Cyril's letters home.

Her relationship with Harold (Whitehouse), often hinted at in Cyril's letters, ended abruptly when Lillian broke off their engagement because she realised that Harold was stifling her independence and free spirit.

Although she had other admirers, Lillian never married, but chose a life devoted to public duty, and caring for her parents.

Although she had been a Baptist for the first 13 years of her life, she chose to join the Anglicans, and her defection was a big blow to her parents when religious differences were far more marked than they are today. Her change of course was mainly due to a desire to spend more time with her friends at St Leonard's Church school where she was one of their ablest scholars. Eventually she became a pupil teacher there herself, specialising in music and needlework.

On her retirement in 1967, her dedication to the teaching profession was rewarded when she was presented with a gold watch from "The County

Borough of Wolverhampton" in recognition of her 56 years of public service.

Lillian joined St Leonard's Parochial Church Council, and after 50 years still in office, she was duly made a life member by the vicar, then the Rev Frank Powell. Until her death at the age of 92 years Lillian was the administrator of the Humphrey Perry charity, annually supplying shoes and clothes for some of the poor children who attended the church school. She was an active member of the Womens' Voluntary Service, and was awarded medals for the work she did on their behalf - and also received medals for her proficiency in the work she did as a member of the British Red Cross Society.

Even as a child it was easy for me to realise what a well known and respected lady I had for an aunt. A simple stroll with her through Bilston town always resulted in the raising of gentlemens' hats, and a chorus of "Good morning Miss Morrell" from the mouths of the very young through to the oldest members of Bilston's inhabitants.

It was Lillian in her wisdom who chose to cherish the precious letters which Cyril wrote to his family members and her obvious love for him was apparent throughout her life.

Thomas Cyril Morrel. Writer of the letters.

Born December 18th 1893.

On leaving school Cyril began work as an apprentice plumber at the firm W H Holden, Bilston. He was well liked and hard working and described by Mr Holden as "a boy with a man's head on his shoulders". He was always keen to learn and willing to please.

It was hoped that having a trade would prevent him from fighting at the front, but all applications for his withdrawal were rejected. He passed the army medicals as A1, despite having a more than slight problem with poor eye-sight, which apparently went undetected.

On reflection Cyril was a perfect example of just one of the thousands of ordinary young men who were sent to their slaughter during the First World War.

Killed March 12th 1917.

Theophillus Morrell.

Born March 26th 1898.

Theo was Cyril's younger brother. It was Cyril's greatest fear that Theo would also be called up to join in the fighting.

Theo trained as an engineer and worked for some time for Harper-Beans at Tipton.

He married Tryphena (Vaney), who is mentioned in Cyril's letters, as she was a lady much admired by both brothers.

Theo and Vaney had one daughter Hilda, who still lives in Bilston now. The family were all active members of Wood St Baptist Chapel where Theo became a deacon.

Sadly Theo also died before his parents on October 9th 1939 at the early age of 41 years after having a heart attack.

Leslie Charles Morrell.

Born October 28th 1899.

The youngest son of the Morrell family. He was the member of the family who was impulsive and quick-tempered, and the young brother Cyril worried about as he was the family member most likely to get into trouble. After the death of his soldier brother Cyril, the young Leslie was determined to seek his revenge on the Germans who had taken his brother's life and therefore ran away to the army barracks in Cannock with the intention of joining up and thus get his opportunity to kill a few of the enemy in retaliation.

Fortunately, although he lied about his age, the authorities found him out and sent for his distressed parents to collect him and return him back to his home. Thus, the only wound Leslie sustained was that of an inoculation scar!

Leslie married a lady called Doris, and they had two children, Enid and Brian. Neither of them now live in Bilston.

Leslie worked for the Wearwell Cycle Company, and died in the 1970's.

Kathleen Nellie Morrell.

Born January 15th 1911.

Kathleen was Cyril's adored little sister who was only 5 years of age when Cyril was called up to join the army. Nearly every letter ended with him sending his love and kisses to her. She was obviously very special to him, and although she was so very young when he disappeared from her life, she has never forgotten him or the affection that he showed to her.

In 1941 Kathleen married Frederick Henry Cross (Harry), who lived for some time in Broad Street, Bilston and whose parents ran a coal business. 'Harry' worked for Cannon Industries, Deepfields, for 43 years and was General Manager for most of that time.

They had three children, Roger, Godfrey and myself, Kathleen, now the present 'keeper' of Cyril's letters.

Kathleen and 'Harry' now live together in a residential home in Goldthorn Hill, Wolverhampton both having reached the age of 89 years.

Why I wanted to record Cyril's letters.

As a child I was always aware of the reverence shown by the older members of my mother's family whenever uncle Cyril came into the conversation.

Discovering the letters upon my parents move into residential care was a great revelation to me and I felt the need to preserve my uncle's words not only as a mark of respect to Cyril but in memory of all the other everyday lads who lost their lives in that terrible war.

For Cyril and all the rest of the boys I felt it my duty to set down his simple words for posterity, they were all heros.

Despite the passage of time we still owe our thanks to those who sacrificed their lives for the preservation of future generations, they should never be forgotten and I am sure that most families in Great Britain, wherever they reside, have their own 'Cyril' to thank somewhere in their histories.